The Ultimate Canada Driver's Handbook

Your Complete Guide to Licensing, Road Rules, and Driving Safely Across Canada

By

Philip Roberts

© **[Philip Roberts].
All rights reserved.**

This driver's handbook is protected by copyright law. No part of this publication may be reproduced, distributed, or transmitted in any form or by any means, including photocopying, recording, or other electronic or mechanical methods, without the prior written permission of the author

Table of contents

Introduction.. 5
    Overview of Canadian Road Rules............ 5
    Licensing Requirements............................. 8
    Road Safety Overview.............................. 11

Chapter 1: Licensing in Canada................. 14
    License Classes in Canada....................... 14
    Steps to Obtain a Driver's License........... 16
    Graduated Licensing System (GLS)......... 19

Chapter 2: Road Signs and Traffic Signals... 23
    Regulatory Signs....................................... 23
    Warning Signs... 26
    Guide Signs.. 28
    Traffic Lights and Pavement Markings..... 30

Chapter 3: Basic Driving Skills....................35
    Starting and Stopping Your Vehicle.......... 35
    Steering Techniques................................. 39
    Safe Following Distance........................... 41

Chapter 4: Understanding Road Rules...... 45
    Speed Limits...45
    Right-of-Way Rules....................................50
    Passing and Lane Changes..................... 54
    Driving in Snow and Ice........................... 59
    Fog, Rain, and Low Visibility.....................64

Emergency Handling................................ 68
Pedestrians and Cyclists.......................... 72
Large Vehicles.. 77
Emergency Vehicles................................. 81

Conclusion.. 85

Chapter 8: Defensive Driving...................... 86

Anticipating Hazards................................ 86
Avoiding Distractions................................ 89
Collision Prevention.................................. 91

Practical Defensive Driving Tips................ 94

Conclusion.. 95

Chapter 9: Roadside Emergencies and Safety.. 97

Handling a Breakdown............................. 97
What to Do After an Accident................... 99
Emergency Equipment Checklist............102
Practical Tips for Roadside Emergencies..... 105
Conclusion.. 106

Chapter 10: Violations, Penalties, and Legal Responsibilities... 108

Speeding and Reckless Driving.............. 108
Driving Under the Influence (DUI)........... 111
Fines and Demerit Points........................ 114
Legal Responsibilities of Drivers............. 116

3

Conclusion..117
Chapter 11: Test Preparation and Practice.... 119
    Sample Knowledge Test Questions........ 119
    Road Test Tips..128
    Glossary of Driving Terms...................... 131
    Province-Specific Rules...........................133
    Resources and Recommended Reading 135
Conclusion..137

Introduction

The introduction to the **Canada Driver's Handbook** serves as a gateway to understanding the essentials of driving within the Canadian landscape. This section provides a foundational overview of the country's road rules, licensing requirements, and the significance of road safety. Whether you're a new driver, a seasoned motorist, or an international visitor, this chapter will equip you with the knowledge to navigate Canada's roads confidently and responsibly.

Overview of Canadian Road Rules

Canada's road network spans over 1.3 million kilometers, making it one of the most extensive in the world. To maintain safety and order, Canada enforces a uniform system of road rules, complemented by provincial and territorial variations. Understanding these rules is crucial for every driver.

Key Features of Canadian Road Rules:

1. **Driving Side:**
   In Canada, vehicles drive on the right-hand side of the road, with overtaking typically done on the left.

2. **Speed Limits:**
   Speed limits are posted in kilometers per hour (km/h) and vary by location:

   - Urban areas: 50 km/h (unless otherwise posted).
   - Rural highways: 80–100 km/h.
   - School and construction zones: 30–50 km/h.

3. **Traffic Signals and Signs:**
   Canadian road signs use

international symbols with bilingual (English and French) labels in some provinces, such as Quebec. Regulatory, warning, and guide signs are color-coded and standardized across the country.

4. **Right-of-Way Rules:**

    - Pedestrians have the right of way at crosswalks.
    - At a four-way stop, the first vehicle to arrive proceeds first.
    - Emergency vehicles always have priority.

5. **Seatbelt and Child Restraint Laws:**

    - Seatbelt use is mandatory for all occupants.
    - Children under a specific weight and height must use an appropriate car seat or booster.

6. **Cell Phone Use:**
   Distracted driving laws prohibit the use of handheld devices while driving. Hands-free options are recommended.

Licensing Requirements

Canada's licensing system is designed to ensure drivers acquire the necessary knowledge, skills, and experience to operate vehicles safely. Licensing requirements vary slightly between provinces and territories but follow a similar structure.

Key Aspects of Licensing in Canada:

1. **Graduated Licensing System (GLS):**
   The GLS is a tiered approach that allows new drivers to gain experience gradually. It typically includes the following stages:

- **Learner's Permit:** Issued after passing a written knowledge test and a vision test. Restrictions include a zero blood alcohol concentration (BAC) limit and mandatory accompaniment by a fully licensed driver.
- **Intermediate License (Probationary):** After passing a road test, drivers receive this license with fewer restrictions. Common rules include no driving between specific hours and limited passengers.
- **Full License:** Granted after completing the probationary period, allowing unrestricted driving.

2. **License Classes:**
Each province categorizes licenses

by vehicle type. For instance:

- Class 5 (or G in Ontario): Standard passenger vehicles.
- Class 1: Tractor-trailers.
- Class 6: Motorcycles.

3. **Requirements for International Drivers:**
Visitors and newcomers can use their valid foreign licenses for a limited period, after which they must apply for a Canadian license. An International Driving Permit (IDP) may also be required.

Road Safety Overview

Road safety is a top priority in Canada, with stringent measures in place to minimize accidents and fatalities. Adhering to safety protocols protects not only the driver but also passengers, pedestrians, and other road users.

Key Road Safety Practices in Canada:

1. **Defensive Driving:**
   Drivers are encouraged to anticipate potential hazards and react appropriately. Defensive driving reduces the risk of collisions and enhances overall safety.

2. **Driving in Adverse Conditions:**
   Canada's diverse climate presents unique challenges. Drivers must be prepared for snow, ice, rain, and fog. Key practices include:

   - Using winter tires in snowy conditions.
   - Maintaining a safe following distance in poor visibility.
   - Reducing speed on wet or icy roads.

3. **Impaired Driving Laws:**
   Canada enforces strict penalties

for driving under the influence of alcohol or drugs. The legal BAC limit is 0.08%, but many provinces have a zero-tolerance policy for new drivers.

4. **Seatbelt and Child Safety:**
 Proper seatbelt use and securing children in appropriate car seats are mandatory to reduce injury risks during accidents.

5. **Awareness Campaigns:**
 Canadian authorities regularly promote road safety through educational campaigns focusing on distracted driving, impaired driving, and speed awareness.

Chapter 1: Licensing in Canada

Understanding Canada's licensing system is critical for anyone planning to drive within the country. Canada's licensing process ensures that drivers possess the necessary knowledge, skills, and experience to operate vehicles safely and responsibly. This chapter covers the classification of licenses, the steps required to obtain a driver's license, and the details of the Graduated Licensing System (GLS) that governs new drivers.

License Classes in Canada

Canada categorizes driver's licenses into classes, each corresponding to specific types of vehicles and their uses. The classification system ensures drivers are trained and tested according to the vehicles they intend to operate.

1. Passenger Vehicle Licenses:

- **Class 5 (or equivalent):**
  This is the standard license for operating passenger vehicles, including cars, SUVs, and light trucks. It also allows drivers to tow trailers within weight limits specified by provincial laws.
- **Class 7 (or equivalent):**
  A learner's or novice driver's license under the Graduated Licensing System.

2. Commercial Vehicle Licenses:

- **Class 1:**
  Allows the operation of semi-trailers and tractor-trailers.
- **Class 2:**
  Permits driving buses designed to carry more than 24 passengers, including school buses.
- **Class 3:**
  Covers large trucks with more than two axles, excluding semi-trailers.

- **Class 4:**
  Authorizes operation of taxis, ambulances, and small buses (e.g., minibuses).

3. Motorcycle Licenses:

- **Class 6 (or equivalent):**
  For motorcycles and mopeds.
- **Class 8 (learner's):**
  A motorcycle learner's license.

4. Special Vehicle Licenses:

- Some provinces require additional endorsements or certifications for vehicles like snowmobiles, farm equipment, or vehicles with air brakes.

Steps to Obtain a Driver's License

The process to obtain a driver's license varies slightly across provinces and territories but generally follows a structured pathway.

Step 1: Research Provincial Requirements

Each province has unique regulations for obtaining a license. For instance, the process in Ontario differs from that in British Columbia or Quebec. Start by visiting the official provincial or territorial transportation authority website.

Step 2: Obtain a Learner's Permit

- **Eligibility:** Applicants must meet the minimum age requirement (usually 16 years old) and pass a vision test.
- **Written Knowledge Test:** Candidates must pass a test on road signs, traffic laws, and safe driving practices. Study guides are available online or through provincial agencies.
- **Conditions:** A learner's permit typically includes restrictions such as no

night driving, no alcohol consumption, and mandatory accompaniment by a fully licensed driver.

Step 3: Practice Driving
Learners must log significant driving experience under various conditions before attempting a road test. Provinces often mandate a specific minimum period for holding a learner's permit.

Step 4: Pass the Road Test

- **Intermediate License:**
  The first road test evaluates basic driving skills. Passing this test grants an intermediate license with fewer restrictions.
- **Full License:**
  After completing the intermediate phase and passing an advanced road test, drivers receive their full license.

Step 5: Renew or Upgrade the License

Licenses must be renewed periodically. Some provinces allow upgrading from a non-commercial to a commercial license after additional testing and training.

Graduated Licensing System (GLS)

The Graduated Licensing System (GLS) is a phased approach designed to help new drivers gain experience and develop safe driving habits over time.

1. Learner's Stage (Class 7 or Equivalent):

- **Eligibility:**
  Minimum age requirements vary but are generally 16 years old.
- **Restrictions:**
    - Zero Blood Alcohol Concentration (BAC).
    - Must drive with a fully licensed supervisor.

- Prohibited from driving between certain hours (e.g., midnight to 5 a.m.).
- **Advancement Criteria:**
  Hold the permit for 6–12 months and pass a basic road test.

2. Intermediate Stage (Class 5 or Equivalent):

- **Purpose:**
  This stage helps drivers transition from supervised to independent driving.
- **Restrictions:**
  - Zero BAC for drivers under a specific age (varies by province).
  - Limit on the number of passengers (e.g., no more than one non-family member under 18).
  - No driving during specific hours in some provinces.
- **Advancement Criteria:**
  Hold the license for 12–24

months and pass an advanced road test.

3. Full License (Class 5 or Equivalent):

- **Eligibility:**
  Drivers must complete the probationary period without violations or accidents.
- **Privileges:**
  - Full driving privileges with no restrictions.
  - Eligibility for additional endorsements (e.g., air brakes, commercial vehicles).

Benefits of the GLS:

- Reduces risks associated with inexperienced drivers.
- Encourages gradual skill development.
- Promotes responsible driving habits.

Chapter 2: Road Signs and Traffic Signals

Road signs and traffic signals play a crucial role in ensuring safe and efficient traffic flow on Canadian roads. These visual cues inform, warn, and guide drivers, helping them make timely and appropriate decisions. Understanding the various categories of road signs, traffic signals, and pavement markings is essential for any driver navigating Canada's roads.

Regulatory Signs

Regulatory signs communicate the rules and regulations that drivers must obey. These signs are typically rectangular or square with white backgrounds and black or red text and symbols. Some may use bold red circles or crosses to emphasize prohibitions.

Key Examples of Regulatory Signs:

1. **Speed Limit Signs:**

    - Display the maximum legal speed in kilometers per hour (e.g., "Speed Limit 50 km/h").
    - Found in urban areas, highways, and school zones.

2. **Stop Signs:**

    - Octagonal red signs with "STOP" written in white.
    - Require drivers to come to a complete stop and yield the right of way before proceeding.

3. **Yield Signs:**

    - Triangular signs with a red border and "YIELD" text.
    - Drivers must slow down and yield the right of way to oncoming traffic.

4. **No Entry Signs:**

- Circular red signs with a white horizontal bar across the center.
- Indicate roads or areas where entry is prohibited.

5. **Parking and Stopping Restrictions:**

    - Signs that specify where parking or stopping is prohibited or restricted.
    - Example: "No Parking," "No Stopping," or time-limited parking.

6. **Turn Restrictions:**

    - Indicate where left turns, right turns, or U-turns are prohibited.
    - Typically use black arrows with red diagonal lines.

7. **Pedestrian Crossings:**

- Alert drivers to pedestrian crossings where vehicles must yield to pedestrians.

Warning Signs

Warning signs alert drivers to potential hazards or changes in road conditions. They are usually diamond-shaped with a yellow background and black text or symbols.

Key Examples of Warning Signs:

1. **Curve and Turn Signs:**

   - Indicate sharp curves or bends ahead.
   - Examples include "Sharp Left Curve" or "Winding Road."
2. **Animal Crossing Signs:**

- Warn drivers of areas where animals like deer or moose are likely to cross.

3. **School Zone Signs:**

    - Highlight areas near schools where drivers should reduce speed and be cautious of children.

4. **Road Surface Conditions:**

    - Warn of slippery surfaces, loose gravel, or bumps.
    - Example: "Slippery When Wet" or "Rough Road."

5. **Lane Changes and Merging:**

    - Indicate merging lanes, lane reductions, or upcoming intersections.

6. **Railway Crossing Signs:**

    - Warn of upcoming railway tracks.

- Often accompanied by flashing lights and barriers.

7. **Traffic Control Ahead:**

    - Indicate upcoming traffic lights, stop signs, or roundabouts.

Guide Signs

Guide signs provide information to help drivers navigate to destinations, identify routes, and find points of interest. These signs are typically rectangular and may use green, blue, or brown backgrounds with white text.

Key Types of Guide Signs:

1. **Route Markers:**

    - Indicate highways or road numbers (e.g., Trans-Canada Highway markers).

    - May include directional arrows to clarify the route.
2. **Destination Signs:**

    - Provide distances to cities, towns, or landmarks.
    - Example: "Toronto – 120 km."
3. **Service Signs:**

    - Blue signs with symbols for services like gas stations, rest areas, hospitals, or accommodations.
4. **Recreational and Cultural Signs:**

    - Brown signs that direct drivers to parks, museums, or historical sites.
5. **Street and Highway Name Signs:**

- Indicate street names, highway exits, or interchanges.
- Often include route numbers or cardinal directions.

Traffic Lights and Pavement Markings

Traffic lights and pavement markings work in conjunction to control the flow of traffic and ensure safety on the roads.

Traffic Lights:

Traffic lights use red, yellow, and green lights to regulate vehicle and pedestrian movement.

1. **Standard Traffic Signals:**

   - **Red Light:** Stop completely before the stop line or crosswalk.
   - **Yellow Light:** Prepare to stop unless it is unsafe to do so.

- **Green Light:** Proceed through the intersection if it is clear.
2. **Flashing Lights:**
   - **Flashing Red Light:** Treat as a stop sign.
   - **Flashing Yellow Light:** Proceed with caution.
3. **Advanced Signals:**
   - Left-turn arrows: Indicate when it is safe to make a protected left turn.
   - Pedestrian signals: Include countdown timers or flashing hand symbols.

Pavement Markings:
 Pavement markings supplement road signs and signals, providing guidance directly on the road surface.

1. **Lane Lines:**

- **White Lines:** Separate lanes moving in the same direction.
- **Yellow Lines:** Separate lanes moving in opposite directions.

2. **Crosswalks:**

- Indicate where pedestrians have the right of way to cross the road.

3. **Stop Lines:**

- Painted white lines at intersections to indicate where vehicles must stop.

4. **Arrows and Symbols:**

- Indicate lane use, such as "turn only" lanes or bicycle lanes.

5. **No-Passing Zones:**

- Solid yellow lines indicate areas where passing is prohibited.
6. **HOV Lanes:**

    - Marked with a diamond symbol and reserved for high-occupancy vehicles.

This comprehensive overview of road signs, traffic signals, and pavement markings ensures drivers are well-equipped to understand and obey the rules of the road. Mastery of these visual cues is essential for safe and confident driving across Canada.

Chapter 3: Basic Driving Skills

Mastering basic driving skills is a fundamental step toward becoming a safe and confident driver. Whether you are a new driver or refreshing your knowledge, understanding the core aspects of vehicle operation is essential. This chapter focuses on three key areas: starting and stopping your vehicle, steering techniques, and maintaining a safe following distance.

Starting and Stopping Your Vehicle

Knowing how to start and stop your vehicle smoothly is a basic yet crucial skill. These actions require a combination of coordination, attention to surroundings, and understanding of your vehicle's controls.

Starting Your Vehicle:

1. **Pre-Drive Checks:**

- Adjust the seat and mirrors for optimal visibility and comfort.
- Fasten your seatbelt and ensure all passengers do the same.
- Check that the parking brake is engaged and the gear is in "Park" (automatic) or "Neutral" (manual).

2. **Starting the Engine:**

- Insert the key into the ignition or press the start button (for keyless systems).
- Press the brake pedal firmly while starting the engine.
- In manual vehicles, press the clutch pedal fully before turning the ignition.

3. **Preparing to Move:**

- Release the parking brake.

- Shift the gear into "Drive" (automatic) or first gear (manual).
- Check mirrors and blind spots to ensure the path is clear.
- Signal your intention to move (e.g., using turn signals).

Stopping Your Vehicle:

1. **Anticipate Stops:**

   - Plan your stops by observing traffic flow, signals, and signs.
   - Begin slowing down gradually to avoid abrupt stops.

2. **Applying Brakes:**

   - Press the brake pedal smoothly and consistently.
   - For manual vehicles, press the clutch pedal

simultaneously to avoid stalling.
3. **Final Stop:**

    - Bring the vehicle to a complete stop behind the stop line, crosswalk, or safe distance from the vehicle ahead.
    - Shift into "Park" (automatic) or neutral (manual) and engage the parking brake.
4. **Exiting the Vehicle Safely:**

    - Turn off the engine and remove the key (if applicable).
    - Check for traffic before opening the door.

Steering Techniques

Steering effectively ensures your vehicle stays under control and follows your intended path. Proper techniques minimize fatigue and improve safety.

1. Hand Position:

- Place your hands on the steering wheel at the "9 and 3 o'clock" positions. This placement provides optimal control and is safer for airbag deployment.
- Avoid holding the wheel at the top or bottom, as it reduces control.

2. Steering Methods:

- **Hand-to-Hand Steering (Push-Pull):**
 This method is used for most driving situations, such as navigating curves or making gentle turns.
    - Push the wheel up with one hand while pulling it down with the other.

- Hands stay on their respective sides, minimizing oversteering.
- **Hand-Over-Hand Steering:** This technique is used for sharp turns or U-turns.
  - One hand crosses over the other while turning the wheel.
  - Provides maximum turning capability in tight spaces.
- **One-Hand Steering:** Reserved for backing up or using vehicle controls like wipers or radios.
  - Place one hand on the wheel at 12 o'clock, but use this method sparingly.

3. **Adjusting Steering Sensitivity:**

- Modern vehicles often have power steering, which requires less effort but may feel more sensitive.
- Practice to understand how much input is needed to steer smoothly.

4. Steering While Reversing:

- Turn the wheel in the direction you want the rear of the vehicle to go.
- Check mirrors and over your shoulder for a clear view of your surroundings.

Safe Following Distance

Maintaining a safe distance from the vehicle ahead is critical to avoiding collisions. The following distance should allow ample time to react to sudden stops or changes in traffic flow.

1. The Three-Second Rule:

- Choose a stationary object (e.g., a road sign or tree) along the road.
- When the vehicle ahead passes the object, begin counting "one thousand one, one thousand two, one thousand three."

- If you pass the object before finishing the count, increase your distance.

2. Adjusting Following Distance:

- **Weather Conditions:** Increase to 4–6 seconds during rain, snow, or fog to account for reduced visibility and longer stopping distances.
- **Heavy Traffic:** In dense traffic, maintain enough space to react to frequent stops and starts.
- **High Speeds:** At highway speeds, extend the following distance to 5–7 seconds, as higher speeds require longer reaction times.

3. Special Situations:

- **Large Vehicles:** Trucks and buses require more stopping distance, so leave additional space.

- **Motorcycles and Bicycles:** These vehicles can stop more quickly than cars; maintain extra caution.
- **Towing Trailers:** Allow more room, as trailers take longer to stop and maneuver.

4. Signs of Tailgating:

- If another vehicle follows too closely, avoid sudden braking. Gradually slow down to encourage them to pass or create space.

5. Emergency Stops:

- Keep your foot ready to brake in high-risk areas, such as intersections or school zones.

Chapter 4: Understanding Road Rules

To drive safely and responsibly on Canadian roads, it is essential to fully understand and comply with the various road rules that govern how traffic flows, how to interact with other drivers, and how to ensure safety at all times. This chapter covers three key areas: speed limits, right-of-way rules, and passing and lane changes. Mastering these rules will help you drive confidently and avoid accidents.

Speed Limits

Speed limits are in place to regulate how fast vehicles can travel on different types of roads, ensuring the safety of all road users. Speed limits are set according to various factors, such as the type of road, traffic conditions, and surrounding environments. Understanding and adhering to speed limits is crucial to preventing accidents and ensuring smooth traffic flow.

1. **Types of Speed Limits:**

   - **Urban Areas (City Streets):**

     - Typically, the speed limit in urban areas is set at 50 km/h unless otherwise posted. This limit is meant to protect pedestrians, cyclists, and other vulnerable road users in busy, high-traffic areas. In school zones, the limit may drop to 30 km/h during school hours.

   - **Residential Areas:**

     - Speed limits in residential neighborhoods are generally set lower, often between 30 km/h and 40 km/h, to protect children playing, pedestrians, and cyclists.

- **Highways and Rural Roads:**

  - The speed limit on most highways is generally set between 90 km/h and 100 km/h, though it may vary based on the specific location, road conditions, and visibility.

- **Expressways and Freeways:**

  - For expressways and freeways, the speed limit usually ranges from 100 km/h to 120 km/h. These roads are designed for higher-speed traffic and typically feature fewer intersections or pedestrian crossings.

- **Construction Zones:**

  - Speed limits in construction zones are often reduced to protect workers and drivers.

These limits can be as low as 40 km/h, depending on the work being done.

- **School Zones:**

  - Speed limits are generally reduced during school hours, often to 30 km/h or lower. These limits are strictly enforced to ensure the safety of children who may be crossing the road.

2. Understanding Speeding Fines and Consequences:

- **Fines:**
  Speeding fines increase with the amount by which you exceed the posted speed limit. Penalties may also include demerit points, which could result in a suspension of your driving privileges if accumulated.

44

- **Speeding in Dangerous Conditions:**
 Driving at excessive speeds in adverse conditions (e.g., during rain, snow, fog, or ice) can result in more severe penalties, as it significantly increases the risk of accidents. Always adjust your speed based on weather and road conditions.

3. Common Misunderstandings about Speed Limits:

- Some drivers may assume that the speed limit is a recommendation, but in reality, it is a legal requirement. Driving above the posted speed limit is a violation of road rules.
- A common misconception is that driving just a few kilometers over the speed limit is harmless. However, even small increases in speed can lead to accidents,

especially in areas with high pedestrian traffic.

Right-of-Way Rules

Right-of-way rules dictate who has the priority to proceed at intersections, pedestrian crossings, and other shared spaces. These rules are designed to prevent confusion, reduce accidents, and ensure smooth traffic flow.

1. At Intersections:

- **Four-Way Stops:**

    - At a four-way stop, the first vehicle to arrive at the intersection has the right of way. If two vehicles arrive simultaneously, the vehicle on the right has the priority.
    - Always come to a complete stop at the stop line and yield to pedestrians.

- **T-intersections:**
  - At a T-intersection, vehicles on the road that ends must yield the right of way to vehicles on the through road.
- **Roundabouts:**
  - Vehicles inside a roundabout have the right of way. When entering, drivers must yield to any traffic already circulating in the roundabout.
- **Traffic Signals:**
  - Obey traffic lights. At green lights, proceed only when the intersection is clear. At red lights, come to a complete stop and wait for the green signal. Yellow signals mean prepare to stop unless doing so would be unsafe.

- **Pedestrian Crossings:**

    - Pedestrians always have the right of way at crosswalks, even when not at intersections. Drivers must stop to allow pedestrians to cross.

2. **When Making Turns:**

- **Left Turns:**

    - When making a left turn, yield to oncoming traffic and pedestrians crossing in the opposite direction. You are required to wait for a gap in traffic before proceeding.

- **Right Turns:**

    - When making a right turn at an intersection, yield to pedestrians crossing in front of your vehicle. On red lights, you may turn right unless posted signs prohibit it, but only after stopping and yielding to other traffic and pedestrians.

- **Yield Signs:**

  - At a yield sign, you must slow down and prepare to stop if necessary. Yield the right of way to vehicles in the lane you are entering or crossing.

3. Emergency Vehicles:

- When an emergency vehicle (e.g., ambulance, fire truck, police) approaches with its lights flashing, pull over to the right side of the road and stop to allow it to pass. Never block an intersection when an emergency vehicle is approaching.

Passing and Lane Changes

Passing and changing lanes are routine maneuvers on the road but must be done safely to avoid collisions. These actions require careful observation of your surroundings, proper signaling, and an understanding of when and where it is legal to pass.

1. When to Pass:

- **On the Left:**

    - In Canada, passing on the left is the standard practice. Before passing, ensure that the road ahead is clear of obstacles or other vehicles. Always signal your intent to pass, check your mirrors and blind spots, and ensure you have enough space to safely move into the left lane.

- **Overtaking at Intersections:**

- It is illegal to pass another vehicle at an intersection or a pedestrian crossing. Wait until you are clear of these areas before overtaking.
- **No-Passing Zones:**
  - These are marked with solid yellow lines, indicating that passing is prohibited for safety reasons. Only pass when you can see clearly ahead and if the road is free from other vehicles, pedestrians, or obstructions.
- **On Highways:**
  - On highways with multiple lanes, overtaking is usually done on the left. However, ensure the lane you are moving into is clear and that you maintain a safe speed while passing.

2. **Lane Changes:**

- **Signaling:**

    - Always signal before changing lanes, indicating your intention to other drivers. Use your mirrors to check for other vehicles in adjacent lanes, and make sure the lane is clear before moving over.

- **Avoid Blind Spots:**

    - Check your vehicle's blind spots (areas not visible in your mirrors) before changing lanes. If necessary, adjust your side mirrors to minimize blind spots.

- **Merging:**

    - When merging onto a highway, yield the right of way to vehicles already traveling in the lane you wish to enter. Use the acceleration lane to match the speed of the highway traffic before merging.

- **Lane Discipline:**

  - Stick to the right lane on multi-lane roads unless you are passing another vehicle. The left lane is typically reserved for passing, and improper use of lanes can result in fines or accidents.

3. Avoiding Dangerous Lane Changes:

- Never change lanes abruptly or without signaling, as this can cause confusion and lead to accidents. Always allow enough time for other drivers to see your intentions and react safely.

Chapter 5: Driving in Special Conditions

Driving in special conditions requires a heightened sense of awareness and the ability to adapt to changes in the road, weather, and environment. The ability to handle challenging driving conditions, such as snow, ice, fog, rain, and emergencies, is crucial for your safety and the safety of others on the road. This chapter will provide comprehensive guidance on how to navigate these conditions effectively and what precautions to take to avoid accidents.

Driving in Snow and Ice

Canada experiences long, cold winters, and snow and ice are common hazards on the roads. Driving in these conditions requires special attention to vehicle handling, road traction, and safety precautions.

1. **Preparing for Winter Driving:**

- **Winter Tires:**
  In snowy and icy conditions, winter tires are essential. They are specifically designed to provide better traction on cold, slippery surfaces and can significantly reduce the risk of accidents. Ensure your tires are properly inflated and have sufficient tread depth.

- **Vehicle Maintenance:**
  Before winter arrives, ensure your vehicle is in optimal condition. Check the battery, brakes, windshield wipers, and antifreeze levels. Make sure your lights are working properly, as snow and ice can obscure visibility, making it essential to have clear headlights and taillights.

2. **Adjusting to Snow and Ice:**

- **Reducing Speed:**
 Snow and ice dramatically reduce traction, making it harder to stop and control your vehicle. Always reduce your speed when driving on these surfaces. Avoid using cruise control, as it can cause the wheels to spin if the road is slick.

- **Braking Techniques:**
 On icy surfaces, it's important to apply brakes gently. If your vehicle has anti-lock brakes (ABS), press the brake pedal firmly and hold it. ABS will pulse the brakes to prevent wheel lock-up. In vehicles without ABS, gently pump the brakes to maintain control. Never slam on the brakes, as this can cause the wheels to lock and result in a loss of control.

- **Staying in Lane:**
 Snow and ice can cause your vehicle to slide, especially during

sharp turns. To maintain control, steer gently and avoid sudden lane changes. If you begin to skid, steer in the direction you want the front of the vehicle to go, and avoid overcorrecting.

- **Stopping on Ice:**
 When coming to a stop on ice, do so gradually. Avoid sudden stops, as this can cause your vehicle to skid. Always increase your following distance, as stopping distances are much longer on slippery surfaces.

3. **Navigating Hills and Slopes:**

- **Going Uphill:**
 When driving uphill on icy or snow-covered roads, avoid excessive acceleration, as this can cause wheel spin. Shift into a lower gear to maintain a steady

pace and gain traction.

- **Going Downhill:**
 When driving downhill, use a lower gear to help slow your vehicle without relying too heavily on the brakes, as they may lock up on icy slopes. Apply brakes gently and in advance of turns.

4. **Avoiding Snowplows:**

- When driving behind a snowplow, maintain a safe distance. Snowplows throw salt, sand, and snow at high speeds, which can damage your vehicle or reduce visibility. Do not attempt to pass a snowplow unless it is safe to do so and visibility is clear.

Fog, Rain, and Low Visibility

Poor visibility due to fog, rain, or other weather conditions requires increased caution and slower driving speeds.

Reduced visibility can make it difficult to spot hazards in time, so adapting to these conditions is essential for safe driving.

1. Driving in Fog:

- **Reduce Speed and Increase Following Distance:** In foggy conditions, visibility can drop to just a few meters. Always reduce your speed and increase the following distance to allow more time for reaction. Use your headlights, but avoid using high beams, as they can reflect off the fog and worsen visibility.

- **Use Fog Lights (if available):** Many vehicles are equipped with fog lights, which are designed to cast a low, wide beam to illuminate the road beneath the fog. Use these lights when driving in dense fog, and turn them off when visibility improves.

- **Maintain Lane Position:**
  Use road markings to help stay in your lane. Avoid sudden movements, and never attempt to pass other vehicles when visibility is limited. If the fog is extremely dense, pull over to a safe location and wait until conditions improve.

2. Driving in Rain:

- **Hydroplaning Prevention:**
  When driving on wet roads, there is a risk of hydroplaning, which occurs when the tires lose contact with the road due to water buildup. To avoid hydroplaning, reduce your speed, especially when there is standing water on the road. If you feel the tires losing traction, gently ease off the accelerator and steer straight.

- **Use of Windshield Wipers:** Ensure your windshield wipers are functioning properly and replace wiper blades regularly. Use your wipers and headlights when it is raining, as rain reduces visibility. On heavy rainfall, it may be necessary to pull over and wait for the rain to subside.

- **Increased Stopping Distance:** Wet roads increase stopping distance. Allow extra space between your vehicle and the one ahead, and avoid hard braking, as it can cause skidding. Brake gently and early to give yourself more time to stop.

3. Driving in Low Visibility (Dusk or Night Driving):

- **Use of Headlights:** Always use your headlights when driving at night or during low-visibility conditions such as dusk, dawn, or heavy rain. Low beams are sufficient for general night driving, but use high beams when driving on dark, rural roads with no other vehicles nearby. Be sure to dim your high beams when approaching other vehicles.

- **Adjusting Your Speed:** When driving at night, your ability to react to hazards is reduced. Drive at a speed that allows you to stop within the distance illuminated by your headlights.

- **Avoiding Glare:** Oncoming headlights can cause glare, which can impair your vision. To reduce glare, look to the right side of the road and avoid staring directly at the headlights. If necessary, use the visor to shield your eyes from bright lights.

Emergency Handling

Even with the utmost caution, unexpected emergencies can occur. Being prepared for emergencies and knowing how to handle them can make all the difference in reducing harm.

1. Tire Blowouts:

- **What to Do:**
  If you experience a tire blowout, keep a firm grip on the steering wheel and avoid panicking. Gradually release the accelerator and let the vehicle slow down naturally. Steer straight and avoid jerking the wheel. Once the vehicle slows down, gently apply the brakes to bring the vehicle to a safe stop. Pull over to the shoulder or a safe area, activate hazard lights, and change the tire or call for roadside assistance.

2. Skidding:

- **What to Do in a Skid:**
  If your vehicle begins to skid, remain calm. Turn the steering wheel in the direction you want the vehicle to go (e.g., if the rear of your vehicle is skidding to the left, steer left). Avoid slamming on the brakes, as this can make the skid worse. If your car has ABS, apply the brakes firmly and steadily. If it does not, pump the brakes gently to regain control.

3. Sudden Stops or Collisions:

- **What to Do After a Collision:**
  If you are involved in an accident, immediately check for injuries and call emergency services. If it is safe, move your vehicle out of traffic to prevent further accidents. Provide assistance to others if necessary and exchange insurance details with the other driver. Avoid

admitting fault at the scene, as this can complicate legal proceedings.

4. Handling Brake Failure:

- **What to Do:**
  If your brakes fail, pump the brake pedal to attempt to build up pressure. If this does not work, use the parking brake gradually to slow the vehicle. Shift into a lower gear to help reduce speed. Finally, steer towards a safe area to bring the vehicle to a stop.

Driving in special conditions can be challenging, but by being prepared, practicing caution, and understanding the proper techniques, you can handle these conditions safely. Always adjust your driving behavior to the circumstances, and never hesitate to pull over or take a break if conditions become too dangerous.

Chapter 6: Sharing the Road

Road safety is not only about how well you control your vehicle but also how well you interact with other road users. Understanding the behaviors and needs of pedestrians, cyclists, large vehicles, and emergency vehicles is essential for ensuring a safe and harmonious driving environment. In this chapter, we will explore the importance of sharing the road with these other users and the best practices for doing so safely.

Pedestrians and Cyclists

Pedestrians and cyclists are some of the most vulnerable road users, especially in urban areas. As a driver, it's essential to be aware of pedestrian and cyclist rights, how to interact with them safely, and how to adjust your driving behavior to minimize risks.

1. Pedestrians:

- **Pedestrian Right-of-Way:** In Canada, pedestrians always have the right of way at marked crosswalks. When you approach a crosswalk, whether there is a pedestrian there or not, you must be prepared to stop. Even at intersections without marked crosswalks, you are expected to yield to pedestrians if they are crossing the road. This is especially true for school zones, where pedestrians—often children—may be crossing the street.

- **Stopping for Pedestrians:** Always stop your vehicle completely if a pedestrian is crossing the road, even if they are not on a designated crosswalk. Never attempt to pass another vehicle that has stopped for a pedestrian, as this can put the pedestrian in danger. When turning at intersections, always be cautious and check for pedestrians who may be crossing the street.

- **School Zones and Crosswalks:**
 In school zones, slow down and watch carefully for children who may be crossing or walking near the road. During the hours of school operation, the speed limit is typically reduced to protect students. Be extra vigilant in areas where children might be present, such as near parks or playgrounds.

- **Pedestrian Crossings:**
 In addition to traditional crosswalks, pedestrian crossings may be equipped with lights or signals. These signals help guide pedestrians and alert drivers to stop when necessary. When approaching a pedestrian-activated signal, you

must stop if the light turns red, giving pedestrians the opportunity to cross safely.

2. **Cyclists:**

- **Cyclist Right-of-Way:**
 Cyclists have the same rights and responsibilities as motorists on the road. They are entitled to use the same lanes and follow the same traffic rules. When passing cyclists, always give them a safe amount of space—at least one meter (three feet) in most jurisdictions. This is especially important when cyclists are riding on busy streets or high-speed roads.

- **Passing Cyclists:**
 When overtaking a cyclist, ensure there is sufficient space between your vehicle and the cyclist to avoid collision. If there is not

enough room to pass safely, wait until you can pass with adequate space. Always signal your intentions, and be aware that cyclists may make sudden maneuvers, such as swerving to avoid obstacles or potholes.

- **Bike Lanes:**
 Many cities and towns have dedicated bike lanes to keep cyclists safe from traffic. When driving, be mindful of these bike lanes and avoid parking or stopping in them. When making turns, always check for cyclists in bike lanes. Cyclists may also make left or right turns at intersections, so always look out for them.

- **Cyclist Visibility:**
 Cyclists are harder to see, especially in low light or adverse weather conditions. Make sure to adjust your driving behavior

accordingly. If you are driving in early morning or evening hours, keep an eye out for cyclists and ensure your headlights are on so that other road users, including cyclists, can see you.

Large Vehicles

Large vehicles such as trucks, buses, and trailers pose a unique challenge to other road users due to their size and weight. These vehicles require additional space and time to maneuver, and their drivers have limited visibility of smaller vehicles. As a driver, it's crucial to understand how to interact with large vehicles safely and be aware of the potential risks.

1. Understanding Blind Spots: Large vehicles, including trucks and buses, have significant blind spots—areas around the vehicle where the driver cannot see smaller vehicles. These blind spots are typically located:

- Directly in front of the vehicle
- On the sides, particularly on the right side of the vehicle
- Behind the vehicle, especially for trailers

When driving near large vehicles, always try to avoid lingering in these blind spots. If you cannot see the driver's mirrors, the driver likely cannot see you. If you need to pass a large vehicle, do so quickly and safely, ensuring you have enough space to move in front of it without cutting it off.

2. Passing Large Vehicles: When passing a large vehicle on a highway or road, do so at a steady speed, maintaining a safe distance. Pass on the left side whenever possible, as trucks have a greater field of vision on their left side. Avoid passing on the right side unless absolutely necessary, as many trucks have a wider right-side blind spot.

- **Increased Stopping Distance:** Large vehicles require a much longer distance to stop, especially when they are fully loaded. Keep this in mind when following behind large vehicles, and maintain a safe following distance. If you are behind a large truck or bus, always allow extra space in case the vehicle needs to stop unexpectedly.

- **Turning and Lane Changes:** Large vehicles have a wider turning radius than smaller vehicles. When turning, these vehicles may need to swing wide to the left or right, sometimes crossing into adjacent lanes. Be cautious and avoid attempting to squeeze past them during turns. Also, avoid driving too closely behind or beside large vehicles when they are changing lanes.

- **Merging and Lane Changes:** Large vehicles need more space to change lanes or merge onto highways. If you are driving alongside a large vehicle and they signal to change lanes, give them extra space to maneuver. Do not try to speed up to pass them or crowd them into a lane. Always be patient and allow the vehicle to complete its maneuver safely.

3. Driving in Adverse Conditions with Large Vehicles:

In poor weather conditions such as heavy rain, snow, or fog, large vehicles may struggle more than smaller vehicles to maintain traction or visibility. Give these vehicles extra space, and reduce your speed to allow for better control of your vehicle. Avoid overtaking a large vehicle in such conditions unless absolutely necessary.

Emergency Vehicles

Emergency vehicles, including ambulances, fire trucks, and police vehicles, are crucial for public safety and often need to navigate traffic quickly to respond to emergencies. As a driver, it's essential to understand how to yield to emergency vehicles and behave appropriately in their presence.

1. Yielding to Emergency Vehicles:

- **Law to Yield:**
  In Canada, drivers are required by law to yield the right of way to emergency vehicles that are using their sirens or flashing lights. When you hear or see an emergency vehicle approaching, you must pull over to the right side of the road and stop. If you are on a multi-lane road, move to the lane farthest to the right, and come to a complete stop.

- **On Highways:**
 On highways, where there are no shoulders or lanes for vehicles to pull over, slow down and move as far to the right as possible. If you cannot pull over, remain in your lane and stop. It's essential to let emergency vehicles pass and ensure there are no obstacles in their path.

- **On Intersections:**
 If an emergency vehicle is approaching an intersection, stop if you are within the intersection. Do not block the intersection, and be prepared to move forward or to the side when it is safe to do so.

2. **Following Emergency Vehicles:**

- **Keep a Safe Distance:**
 After you've yielded to an emergency vehicle, do not follow it too closely. Keep a safe distance to

avoid obstructing the path of the emergency vehicle or causing any distractions. Generally, maintain at least 150 meters (500 feet) of distance behind emergency vehicles when they are responding to calls.

- **Do Not Attempt to Overtake:** Never attempt to pass an emergency vehicle, even if you are on a multi-lane road or if it appears to be moving slowly. Emergency vehicles often have to maneuver through traffic, and passing them can obstruct their path or put you in a dangerous situation.

3. Emergency Vehicle Locations: Emergency vehicles can be found in various locations, including residential neighborhoods, commercial areas, and along highways. Be especially vigilant when driving near hospitals, fire stations, and police stations, as emergency vehicles may be responding to incidents in these areas.

Conclusion

Sharing the road with pedestrians, cyclists, large vehicles, and emergency vehicles requires awareness, patience, and respect. Each road user has unique needs and risks associated with their presence on the road. As a responsible driver, your ability to interact safely with these other users ensures not only your safety but also the safety of everyone around you. By following the rules of the road and making considerate decisions, you contribute to a safer driving environment for all.

Chapter 8: Defensive Driving

Defensive driving is a skill that focuses on anticipating potential road hazards, avoiding distractions, and taking proactive measures to prevent collisions. By practicing defensive driving, you can reduce risks, ensure safety, and handle unpredictable situations effectively. In this chapter, we will explore the core principles of defensive driving, including anticipating hazards, avoiding distractions, and preventing collisions.

Anticipating Hazards

Anticipating hazards is the cornerstone of defensive driving. It involves staying alert, reading the road, and predicting potential risks before they occur. Here are the key strategies:

1. Scan the Road Ahead:

- Continuously scan the road ahead, including your lane, adjacent

lanes, and intersections. Look for potential obstacles, erratic drivers, or changes in road conditions.
- Use the "12-second rule" to keep your eyes focused on where your vehicle will be in 12 seconds. This allows you to identify and react to hazards early.

2. Check Mirrors Frequently:

- Regularly check your rearview and side mirrors to stay aware of surrounding traffic.
- Be mindful of vehicles in your blind spots, especially when merging or changing lanes.

3. Recognize Hazardous Areas:

- **Intersections:** These are high-risk areas where collisions are more likely to occur. Slow down, yield the right-of-way when necessary, and look out for vehicles running red lights or stop signs.

- **Highway Entrances and Exits:** Watch for merging vehicles and adjust your speed or lane position to accommodate them.

4. Watch for Unpredictable Drivers:

- Keep a safe distance from drivers who are speeding, weaving between lanes, or showing signs of impaired driving.
- Be extra cautious around drivers who are distracted, such as those using their phones or eating while driving.

5. Adjust to Weather Conditions:

- In adverse weather conditions like rain, snow, or fog, reduce your speed and increase your following distance.
- Use your headlights appropriately and be prepared for reduced visibility and slippery roads.

Avoiding Distractions

Distractions are a leading cause of collisions, making it essential to minimize anything that takes your attention away from the road. Defensive drivers prioritize focus and control while driving.

1. Common Types of Distractions:

- **Visual Distractions:** Taking your eyes off the road, such as looking at a phone or GPS.
- **Manual Distractions:** Taking your hands off the wheel, such as eating, drinking, or adjusting the radio.
- **Cognitive Distractions:** Letting your mind wander, such as daydreaming or being preoccupied with personal issues.

2. Tips for Avoiding Distractions:

- **Put Away Electronic Devices:** Turn off your phone or set it to

"Do Not Disturb" mode while driving. If you need to use GPS, program it before you start driving.

- **Plan Ahead:**
 Adjust your mirrors, seat, and climate controls before you start driving. This prevents the need to make adjustments while on the move.
- **Limit Conversations:**
 Keep conversations with passengers to a minimum and avoid emotional or intense discussions that could divert your focus.

3. Managing Fatigue:

- Avoid driving when tired, as fatigue reduces reaction times and impairs judgment.
- Take regular breaks on long trips to stay alert and refreshed.

Collision Prevention

Collision prevention is the ultimate goal of defensive driving. By staying proactive and adopting safe driving practices, you can minimize the likelihood of accidents.

1. Maintain a Safe Following Distance:

- Use the "three-second rule" to ensure you have enough space between your vehicle and the one in front of you. Increase this to five or six seconds in poor weather or heavy traffic.
- Avoid tailgating, as it reduces your ability to react to sudden stops or changes in traffic flow.

2. Be Cautious When Changing Lanes:

- Always use your turn signal to indicate your intentions.

- Check your mirrors and blind spots before merging into another lane.
- Avoid abrupt lane changes and be mindful of other drivers who may not be following proper lane-change etiquette.

3. Obey Speed Limits:

- Driving at an appropriate speed for the conditions is critical. Speeding reduces your ability to react to hazards and increases stopping distances.
- In areas with heavy pedestrian activity, such as school zones, drive well below the posted speed limit to ensure safety.

4. Plan for the Unexpected:

- Assume other drivers may make mistakes and be prepared to react accordingly.

- If a vehicle cuts you off, avoid aggressive responses like honking or tailgating. Instead, adjust your speed and focus on maintaining a safe distance.

5. Stay in Control During Emergencies:

- If your brakes fail, pump the brake pedal to build up pressure or use the emergency brake.
- In the event of a tire blowout, hold the steering wheel firmly, slow down gradually, and pull over to a safe area.
- When skidding, steer in the direction you want the front of your vehicle to go and avoid slamming on the brakes.
-

Practical Defensive Driving Tips

1. **Stay Calm and Patient:**

- Defensive driving requires patience and a calm attitude. Avoid road rage or aggressive driving behaviors that can escalate situations.

2. **Use Headlights Wisely:**

    - Use low beams in foggy conditions and high beams only when driving in areas with low visibility and no oncoming traffic.

3. **Anticipate Pedestrians and Cyclists:**

    - Slow down near crosswalks, schools, and areas with heavy pedestrian or cyclist activity.

4. **Be Prepared for the Unexpected:**

    - Always have an emergency kit in your car, including items like a flashlight, first aid supplies, and reflective triangles.

Conclusion

Defensive driving is a proactive approach to road safety that helps drivers anticipate and respond to potential hazards. By staying alert, avoiding distractions, and practicing collision prevention strategies, you can navigate Canada's roads confidently and safely. Adopting these practices not only reduces the risk of accidents but also contributes to a safer driving environment for everyone.

Chapter 9: Roadside Emergencies and Safety

Roadside emergencies can happen unexpectedly, and being prepared can make a significant difference in managing these situations effectively. This chapter provides detailed guidance on handling vehicle breakdowns, responding to accidents, and ensuring you have the necessary emergency equipment for safe and responsible driving.

Handling a Breakdown

A vehicle breakdown can be stressful and potentially dangerous, especially on busy roads or in adverse weather. Follow these steps to manage the situation safely:

1. Signal and Pull Over Safely:

- If you sense a mechanical issue or experience a breakdown, turn on

your hazard lights immediately to alert other drivers.
- Gradually reduce your speed and steer your vehicle to the side of the road or the nearest safe location, such as the shoulder or an emergency lane.
- Avoid stopping on curves, near blind spots, or in high-traffic areas to minimize risk.

2. Secure Your Vehicle:

- Once stopped, engage the parking brake and shift the vehicle into park (or neutral if driving a manual transmission).
- If you suspect an engine fire, do not open the hood; exit the vehicle and move to a safe distance.

3. Make Yourself Visible:

- Turn on your hazard lights and use reflective triangles or flares to

warn other drivers of your presence.
- If it is safe, raise the hood of your vehicle as a universal signal of a breakdown.

4. Stay Inside the Vehicle When Necessary:

- If the breakdown occurs on a busy highway or in an unsafe area, remain inside your vehicle with your seatbelt fastened until help arrives.

5. Call for Assistance:

- Use your phone to call roadside assistance or local authorities if needed. Be prepared to provide your location and describe the issue.

What to Do After an Accident

Accidents can be overwhelming, but knowing the proper steps to take can ensure safety, compliance with the law, and proper documentation for insurance claims.

1. Ensure Safety First:

- If possible, move vehicles involved in the accident to the side of the road to prevent further collisions.
- Turn on hazard lights and set up warning devices such as reflective triangles to alert approaching traffic.

2. Check for Injuries:

- Assess yourself, passengers, and other involved parties for injuries.
- Call emergency services immediately if anyone is injured or if there is significant vehicle damage.

3. Notify Authorities:

- In Canada, accidents involving injuries, significant property

damage, or impaired driving must be reported to the police.
- If the accident is minor, exchange information with the other driver but still consider reporting it to local authorities for record purposes.

4. Exchange Information:

- Collect the following information from all involved parties:
  - Names, addresses, and contact details.
  - Driver's license numbers.
  - Insurance company names and policy numbers.
  - Vehicle make, model, and license plate numbers.

5. Document the Scene:

- Take clear photos or videos of the accident scene, including vehicle positions, damages, and road conditions.

- Write down details of the incident, including time, location, and a brief description of what occurred.

6. File an Insurance Claim:

- Contact your insurance company as soon as possible to report the accident and initiate the claims process.
- Provide all necessary documentation, including photos and the police report, if applicable.

Emergency Equipment Checklist

Carrying the right emergency equipment ensures you are prepared for various roadside situations. Below is a comprehensive checklist of items to include in your vehicle:

1. Visibility and Warning Devices:

- Reflective triangles or road flares.
- High-visibility safety vest.

2. Tools and Equipment:

- Spare tire, jack, and lug wrench.
- Jumper cables or a portable battery booster.
- Basic tool kit (e.g., screwdrivers, pliers, wrenches).
- Duct tape and multipurpose utility knife.

3. Safety Essentials:

- Flashlight with extra batteries.
- First aid kit (including bandages, antiseptic, and pain relievers).
- Fire extinguisher designed for automotive use.

4. Weather-Specific Items:

- Ice scraper and snow brush for winter conditions.
- Blanket and gloves for cold weather.
- Sunscreen and water for hot weather.

5. Communication and Navigation:

- Fully charged phone or portable charger.
- Paper maps in case of GPS failure.

6. Emergency Supplies:

- Bottled water and non-perishable snacks.
- Emergency whistle to signal for help.
- Cash or coins for payphones or tolls.

7. Documentation:

- Vehicle owner's manual.
- Proof of insurance and registration.
- Emergency contact numbers.
-

Practical Tips for Roadside Emergencies

1. **Stay Calm:**

- Panicking can cloud your judgment. Take deep breaths and focus on solving the problem.

2. **Know Your Vehicle:**

    - Familiarize yourself with your car's emergency features, such as the location of the spare tire and how to use the jack.

3. **Be Prepared for Weather Changes:**

    - Canada's weather can be unpredictable, so always be prepared for conditions such as snow, rain, or extreme cold.

4. **Regular Maintenance:**

    - Preventive maintenance reduces the likelihood of breakdowns. Regularly check your tires, brakes, and fluid levels.

Conclusion

Roadside emergencies require a calm and methodical approach to ensure safety and resolution. Whether dealing with a breakdown, an accident, or equipping your vehicle with emergency essentials, being prepared is key. By following the guidelines outlined in this chapter, you can confidently handle unexpected situations and minimize risks for yourself and others on the road.

Chapter 10: Violations, Penalties, and Legal Responsibilities

Understanding the legal framework governing driving in Canada is essential to maintaining safety and avoiding severe consequences. Violations such as speeding, reckless driving, and driving under the influence (DUI) not only jeopardize lives but also come with substantial penalties. This chapter will provide an in-depth analysis of common traffic violations, the associated penalties, and the legal responsibilities of Canadian drivers.

Speeding and Reckless Driving

Speeding
 Speeding is one of the most common traffic violations in Canada. It occurs when a driver exceeds the posted speed limit or drives too fast for prevailing conditions, such as bad weather or heavy traffic.

1. Speed Limits in Canada:

- Urban areas: Typically 50 km/h unless otherwise posted.
- School zones: Generally 30-40 km/h during school hours.
- Rural highways: Usually 80-100 km/h depending on the province.
- Construction zones: Reduced speed limits are strictly enforced.

2. Consequences of Speeding:

- **Fines:** The amount varies by province but increases with the severity of the violation. For example, in Ontario, speeding 1-19 km/h over the limit may result in a fine of $2.50 per km/h, while speeding 50 km/h or more can lead to fines exceeding $2,000.
- **Demerit Points:** Speeding violations typically result in demerit points on your driving record. Accumulating too many

points may lead to license suspension.
- **Insurance Implications:** Speeding tickets can increase insurance premiums significantly.

Reckless Driving

Reckless driving is a more severe offense involving actions that display a willful disregard for the safety of others. Examples include excessive speeding, street racing, and dangerous lane changes.

1. Legal Definition:

- Reckless driving is typically defined as behavior that endangers lives or property. This offense is taken seriously and can result in both civil and criminal penalties.

2. Penalties for Reckless Driving:

- Heavy fines ranging from hundreds to thousands of dollars.

- Immediate license suspension or revocation.
- Potential imprisonment, depending on the severity and consequences of the reckless behavior.

Driving Under the Influence (DUI)

Driving under the influence of alcohol or drugs is one of the most dangerous and heavily penalized traffic violations in Canada.

1. Legal Blood Alcohol Concentration (BAC) Limits:

- The legal BAC limit for most drivers is 0.08%.
- In some provinces, drivers with a BAC of 0.05% or higher may face administrative penalties.
- Novice drivers or those under 21 often face a zero-tolerance policy,

meaning no alcohol is permitted in their system while driving.

2. Drug-Impaired Driving:

- The legalization of cannabis in Canada has led to stricter measures against drug-impaired driving.
- Police use roadside oral fluid drug screening devices to detect THC, the psychoactive component in cannabis.

3. Consequences of DUI:

- **Immediate Penalties:** Police may issue a roadside suspension, impound the vehicle, or demand mandatory breathalyzer tests.
- **Fines and Charges:**
    - First offense: Fines starting at $1,000.
    - Repeat offenses: Heavier fines, mandatory education

programs, and potential jail time.
- **License Suspension:**
  - Immediate suspension of 90 days for first offenses.
  - Longer suspensions for subsequent offenses, which could last years.
- **Ignition Interlock Device:**
  - Repeat offenders may be required to install a device that prevents the vehicle from starting if alcohol is detected on the driver's breath.

4. **Long-Term Consequences:**

- Criminal record that could affect employment and travel.
- Substantial increases in insurance premiums.

Fines and Demerit Points

Fines and demerit points serve as deterrents for traffic violations and encourage compliance with road rules.

1. Fines:

- Issued based on the severity of the violation and provincial regulations.
- Payment deadlines must be met to avoid additional penalties, such as late fees or license suspension.

2. Demerit Points:

- Each province has its own system for demerit points, which are assigned for specific traffic offenses.
- Examples of demerit points include:
    - Speeding: 3-6 points.
    - Failure to yield: 3 points.
    - Running a red light: 2-3 points.

- Points remain on your driving record for a specified period (typically two years).

3. Consequences of Accumulating Demerit Points:

- A warning letter may be issued after reaching a certain threshold of points.
- License suspension can occur if the maximum allowable points are exceeded. For example:
    - Ontario: Suspension at 15 points for fully licensed drivers.
    - Quebec: Suspension at 15 points for drivers under 23, 30 points for drivers aged 24-34, and 35 points for drivers 35 and older.

Legal Responsibilities of Drivers

1. Know the Laws:

- Drivers must understand and comply with provincial and federal traffic laws. Ignorance of the law is not a valid excuse for violations.

2. Ensure Vehicle Safety:

- Regularly maintain your vehicle to ensure it is roadworthy.
- Check that lights, brakes, and tires meet safety standards.

3. Carry Necessary Documentation:

- Drivers must have a valid driver's license, vehicle registration, and proof of insurance while driving.

4. Report Accidents:

- Drivers involved in collisions must report accidents to the police if there are injuries, fatalities, or significant property damage.

5. Responsibility to Pedestrians and Cyclists:

- Yield the right-of-way at crosswalks and ensure the safety of vulnerable road users.

Conclusion

Traffic violations, whether minor or severe, can have serious consequences for drivers in Canada. Understanding the rules, penalties, and legal responsibilities is essential for maintaining a clean driving record and contributing to road safety. By adhering to the principles outlined in this chapter, drivers can avoid violations, reduce risks, and ensure responsible behavior behind the wheel.

Chapter 11: Test Preparation and Practice

Preparing for your Canadian driver's test is a crucial step in obtaining your license. This chapter provides comprehensive guidance on excelling in both the written knowledge test and the practical road test. By familiarizing yourself with sample questions and applying expert road test tips, you'll increase your chances of success and gain confidence as a driver.

Sample Knowledge Test Questions

The knowledge test assesses your understanding of traffic laws, road signs, and safe driving practices. Below are 20 sample questions to help you prepare effectively.

1. What does a solid yellow line on your side of the road mean?

- A. You may pass if it is safe.

- B. You must not pass.
- C. Passing is allowed in all conditions.
- D. Passing is only allowed in residential areas.

   Answer: B

2. Who has the right of way at a four-way stop?

- A. The first vehicle to arrive.
- B. The vehicle on the right, if two vehicles arrive simultaneously.
- C. Both A and B.
- D. The vehicle with the larger size.

   Answer: C

3. What should you do if you see a school bus with flashing red lights?

- A. Pass the bus carefully.
- B. Stop at least 20 meters away.
- C. Slow down and proceed cautiously.

- D. Stop only if children are crossing.
  Answer: B

4. What does a flashing yellow traffic light mean?

- A. Stop and wait for green.
- B. Proceed with caution.
- C. Yield to pedestrians only.
- D. Treat it as a red light.
  Answer: B

5. When approaching a pedestrian crosswalk, you must:

- A. Stop only if pedestrians are already crossing.
- B. Slow down and honk your horn.
- C. Yield to pedestrians whether or not they are crossing.
- D. Continue driving if no pedestrians are visible.
  Answer: C

6. What does a white diamond symbol on the road indicate?

- A. Reserved lanes for high-occupancy vehicles (HOV).
- B. Dangerous curves ahead.
- C. A merging lane.
- D. A lane for bicycles only.
Answer: A

7. How far must you park from a fire hydrant?

- A. 1 meter.
- B. 3 meters.
- C. 5 meters.
- D. 10 meters.
Answer: B

8. When should you use your high-beam headlights?

- A. At all times during nighttime driving.
- B. When driving in fog.
- C. On open roads with no oncoming traffic.
- D. In residential areas.
Answer: C

9. If your vehicle starts to skid, you should:

- A. Brake immediately.
- B. Steer in the opposite direction of the skid.
- C. Steer in the direction you want to go.
- D. Accelerate to regain control.
  Answer: C

10. What should you do if you encounter an emergency vehicle with flashing lights?

- A. Continue driving normally.
- B. Pull over to the right and stop.
- C. Speed up to clear the way.
- D. Pull over only if the vehicle is behind you.
  Answer: B

11. How often should you check your mirrors while driving?

- A. Every 30 seconds.
- B. Every 5-8 seconds.

- C. Only when changing lanes.
- D. Only when braking.
   Answer: B

12. What is the purpose of a roundabout?

- A. To allow U-turns.
- B. To reduce traffic speed and increase safety.
- C. To bypass traffic lights.
- D. To allow only right turns.
   Answer: B

13. When can you make a right turn at a red light?

- A. Always, without stopping.
- B. Only when there is no "No Right Turn on Red" sign.
- C. Only at intersections with no traffic.
- D. Never.
   Answer: B

14. What should you do if your brakes fail while driving?

- A. Pump the brakes repeatedly.
- B. Shift to a lower gear.
- C. Use the emergency brake.
- D. All of the above.
   Answer: D

15. What does a yellow sign with a black arrow mean?

- A. No entry.
- B. Curve ahead.
- C. Dead end.
- D. Steep hill.
   Answer: B

16. When driving in fog, you should use:

- A. High-beam headlights.
- B. Low-beam headlights.
- C. Hazard lights.
- D. No lights.
   Answer: B

17. What should you do at a railway crossing with flashing lights?

- A. Stop at least 5 meters from the tracks.
- B. Proceed cautiously.
- C. Ignore the lights if no train is visible.
- D. Speed up to cross quickly.

Answer: A

18. How close can you follow another vehicle in ideal driving conditions?

- A. 1 car length.
- B. 2 seconds behind the vehicle.
- C. 5 seconds behind the vehicle.
- D. Any distance if you can stop in time.

Answer: B

19. What is the penalty for not wearing a seatbelt?

- A. A warning.
- B. A fine and potential demerit points.

- C. Suspension of your driver's license.
- D. No penalty.

    Answer: B

20. Who is responsible for ensuring passengers under 16 wear seatbelts?

- A. The driver.
- B. The passengers themselves.
- C. The police officer.
- D. The parent or guardian.

    Answer: A

Road Test Tips

The road test evaluates your ability to apply safe driving practices and follow road rules. These tips will help you prepare:

1. Practice Common Maneuvers:

- Master skills such as parallel parking, three-point turns, and merging.
- Practice in areas with similar road conditions to the test location.

2. Know Your Test Route:

- Familiarize yourself with the test route, including school zones, intersections, and roundabouts.

3. Prepare Your Vehicle:

- Ensure your car is in good condition with functioning lights, brakes, and signals.
- Adjust mirrors and seat positions before starting the test.

4. Drive Defensively:

- Always check mirrors and blind spots before lane changes or turns.
- Maintain safe following distances and obey speed limits.

5. Stay Calm and Confident:

- Listen carefully to the examiner's instructions.
- Take deep breaths to manage nerves.

6. Avoid Critical Errors:

- Failing to stop at stop signs or yield to pedestrians can result in immediate failure.
- Avoid distractions, such as looking at your phone or excessive talking.

7. Review Common Mistakes:

- Not checking mirrors frequently.
- Rolling stops at stop signs.
- Failure to signal appropriately.

8. Be Courteous:

- Yield to other drivers, pedestrians, and cyclists when required.
- Demonstrate patience and respect for road users.

Appendix

The appendix provides valuable supplementary information to enhance your understanding of driving in Canada. It includes a glossary of essential driving terms, province-specific rules to guide drivers in various jurisdictions, and a curated list of resources and recommended reading materials for continued learning.

Glossary of Driving Terms

This glossary defines key terms used in the handbook and throughout Canada's driving regulations:

- **Blind Spot:** An area around your vehicle that cannot be seen in the mirrors and requires a shoulder check to ensure no vehicles or pedestrians are present.

- **Defensive Driving:** A driving approach that focuses on anticipating potential hazards and taking proactive measures to avoid accidents.
- **Demerit Points:** Penalties added to a driver's record for violations. Accumulating too many points can lead to license suspension.
- **Graduated Licensing System (GLS):** A step-by-step process for new drivers to obtain full driving privileges.
- **High-Occupancy Vehicle (HOV) Lane:** A reserved lane for vehicles with a minimum number of occupants, such as carpoolers.
- **Right-of-Way:** The legal right to proceed before other road users in a specific situation, such as at intersections or crosswalks.
- **Yield:** To slow down or stop to allow another vehicle, pedestrian, or cyclist to proceed.

Province-Specific Rules

Each Canadian province has unique driving laws and requirements. Here are highlights for some major provinces:

1. Ontario:

- **Speed Limits:** Maximum speed on highways is typically 100 km/h unless otherwise posted.
- **Winter Tires:** Not mandatory but highly recommended for winter driving conditions.
- **Cell Phone Use:** Strictly prohibited without a hands-free device.

2. British Columbia:

- **Speed Limits:** Maximum speed on highways can reach 120 km/h in designated areas.

- **Road Tests:** Two stages: Class 7L (Learner) and Class 7 (Novice) before obtaining a Class 5 license.
- **Impaired Driving:** Zero tolerance for drivers in the GLS.

3. **Alberta:**

- **Speed Limits:** Maximum highway speed is 110 km/h unless posted otherwise.
- **Mandatory Insurance:** All vehicles must have at least third-party liability coverage.
- **Passing Cyclists:** Minimum distance of 1 meter required.

4. **Quebec:**

- **Winter Tires:** Mandatory from December 1 to March 15.
- **Alcohol Limits:** Lower threshold for novice and professional drivers.

- **Road Signs:** Unique symbols often bilingual in French and English.

5. Manitoba:

- **Graduated Licensing:** Features three stages: Learner, Intermediate, and Full.
- **Wildlife Hazards:** Increased risk on rural highways; drivers must exercise caution.

Resources and Recommended Reading

Official Driver's Handbooks by Province:

- Access detailed guides for each province, available online or at local licensing offices. Examples include:
    - *Ontario Official Driver's Handbook.*
    - *ICBC Driving Guide (British Columbia).*

Driving Safety Courses:

- Many provinces offer defensive driving and winter driving courses to improve safety and skills.

Websites and Apps:

- **Transport Canada:** Official government site with driving laws and updates.
- **DriveTest (Ontario):** Resources for licensing and road test booking.
- **ICBC (British Columbia):** Practice knowledge tests and road safety tips.

Online Tutorials:

- Platforms like YouTube feature tutorials on parallel parking, road test preparation, and winter driving techniques.

Emergency Driving Tools:

- Download apps like Waze or Google Maps for real-time navigation and traffic updates.
- Invest in emergency roadside kits available at automotive stores or online.

Conclusion

The appendix is a valuable resource for Canadian drivers to clarify terms, adapt to province-specific requirements, and access further learning tools. By utilizing this section, drivers can deepen their knowledge and ensure safe, responsible road use across Canada.

Printed in Dunstable, United Kingdom